# WHEN THE AARDVARK PARKED ON THE ARK

# CALVIN MILLER

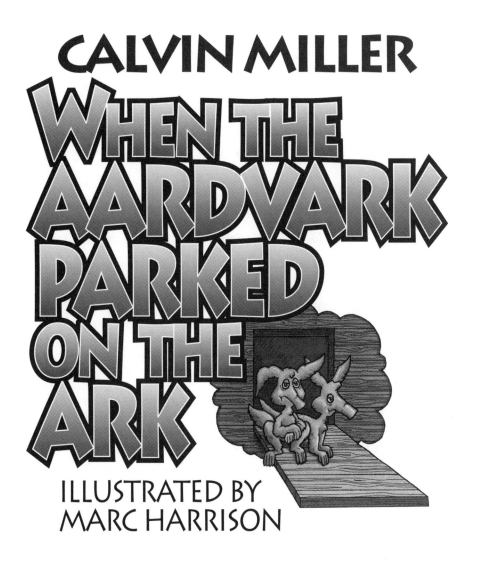

# WHEN THE AARDVARK PARKED ON THE ARK

ILLUSTRATED BY
MARC HARRISON

WORD PUBLISHING
Dallas•London•Vancouver•Melbourne

WHEN THE AARDVARK PARKED ON THE ARK

Cover Design by Dennis Davidson.
Cover Illustration by Marc Harrison.

**Library of Congress Cataloging-in-Publication Data**

Miller, Calvin.
    When the aardvark parked on the ark / Calvin Miller ; illustrations by Marc Harrison.
       p.  cm.
    "Word kids!"
    Summary: Whimsical verses present wisdom from the Bible and advice for living in the real world.
    ISBN 0-8499-3699-3
    1. Children's poetry, American. 2. Christian poetry, American. [1. Christian life—Poetry.] I. Harrison, Marc, ill.  II. Title.
PS3563.I376W48   1995
811'.54—dc20
                                  95-13082
                                        CIP
                                        AC

*Printed in the United States of America*

95 96 97 98 99 00  LBM  9 8 7 6 5 4 3 2 1

*For my grandson Jared Daniel Sloger*

# THE SAWED-OFF SEESAW

You cannot have fun on a sawed-off seesaw
The best seesaws always go
Seesaw,
Seesaw,
Seesaw.
And seesaws that never are fun go,
Seeeeeee-saw, Bump,
Seeeeeee-saw, Bump,
Seeeeeee-saw, Bump!

In life or on seesaws
good balance is key.
To zoom up and down
And enjoy your ride
Be sure that your board
Is the same on both sides.
When you push with your ankles
And lift with your knees,
Your "saws" must be
Just as long as your "sees,"
Or else, you'll be sitting
Quite flat on the ground
Or so very far up
That you'll never get down.
In life or on seesaws,
There's ground and there's air
But a lop-sided seesaw
Will get you nowhere.

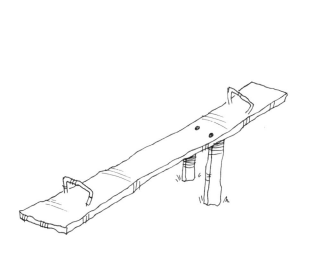

## IF THERE WERE NO "B'S"

If there were no "B's," it sure would be sad.
We'd have to ride "ikes" and sleep in our "eds."
And kids who played trumpets would play in the "and."
We'd eat our "ham-urgers" at "ham-urger" stands.
At ice cream cafes
Eating "utterscotch" sundaes
And "anana" splits
So utterly " 'affled,"
We'd just sit and sit.
All hares would be "unnies."
(It sure would sound funny)
And sweet little "a'ies"
Would not seem so huggy.
Their mothers would stroll them
In "lack" "a'y" "uggies."
If muscles were "iceps"
And minds were all "rains"
We'd all hit an "ase-all"
Or play with our trains,
And carry "um-rellas"
To keep off the rains.

We'd have to ride "uses"
And "uckle" our "oots"
And "utton" our "lazers"
Down over our suits.
And sweet little "irds"
Would fly as "irds" do
High in the sky
Where the skies are quite "lue."

Ever since I was "orn"
I was thankful for skies
And good "ooks" and "row-oats"
And "straw-erry" pies,
Chocolate milkshakes and "ras-erry" freezes
And maples and oaks and "mul-erry" trees.
"Ut" mostly I'm thankful
Whenever I please
To use hundreds and hundreds
And hundreds of "B's."

## LEONARDO LOBSTER

It was senseless, but Leonardo kept charging the cage.
He was caught in a trap and he swam in a rage.
He knew he was done for and soon would be dead
When he suddenly thought what his father once said.

"If ever you enter a trap, Leonardo, you don't have
To find yourself stewed, baked, and dead.
You can't fight the trap, my two-pincered son,
By charging the steel that lies out ahead."

Leonardo grew calm and quit charging ahead.
His BB-like eyes raised up from his head.

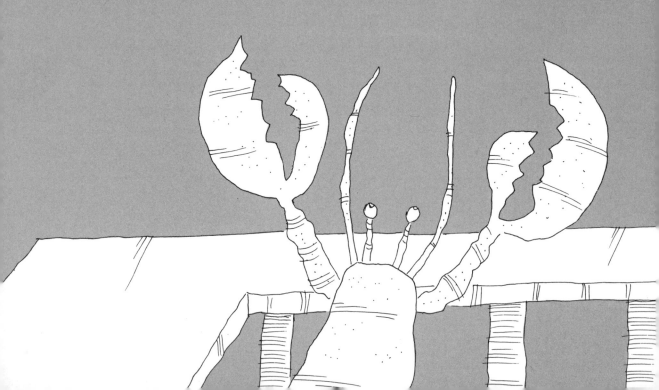

He looked at the floor of his trap for a door
And clearly could see there was none.
But as he swam up to the top of his cell
He found the small window through which he fell.
He swam swiftly up, and rid of his rage,
He soon found himself outside of his cage.

"The reason all lobsters wind up in pails, with
Elegant people eating their tails,
Is that they don't try enough different ways
To escape from the prisons of men.
It does little good when you know you are caught
To keep charging at walls, again and again."

Leonardo became a great liberator.
He moved through the
traps and swam without fear.
Whenever he saw a brother entrapped,
He was careful, but unafraid to swim near.
"Look up, look up!" He would cry through the
Gloom, "Or this trap where you struggle
Will soon be your tomb.
The reason all lobsters wind up in pails, with
Elegant people eating their tails,
Is that they don't try enough different ways
To escape from the prisons of men.
It does little good when you know you are caught
To keep charging at walls, again and again.
Look up! Look up! Look up!"

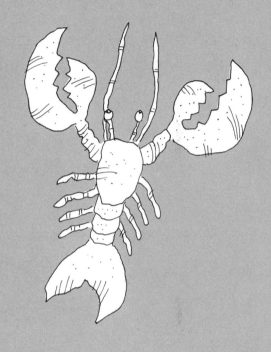

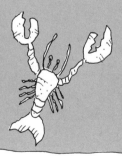

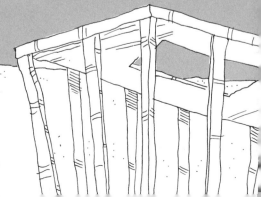

## A GLUTTON CAN'T BUTTON HIS SHIRT

There's literally nuttin' a glutton won't eat.
He'll butter his mutton and pepper his meat.
He'll eat every roll that is left in the dish.
And pick every morsel of meat from his fish.
He'll eat a whole roast and three baked potatoes
A chicken or two and a sack of tomatoes
And then when he's finished a twenty-inch pie,
He will tell you he's hungry and must eat or die.
And he'll buy a larger shirt.

There's literally nuttin' a glutton won't eat.
From elephant trunks to a piggy-wigs feet,
He'll grab for the crackers and pickles and dill
And porridge and tacos and fish eggs and swill
And tree-frogs and shark-ears and crocodile eggs
And sugar-shell ants and centipede legs.
He'll eat his bananas by munching a bunch
And then promptly ask, "What time is our lunch?"
And he'll buy an extra-large shirt.

There's literally nuttin' a glutton won't eat,
A turnip or parsnip or freshly dug beet,
Honey-dipped locusts and fudge-covered leeks,
And anything else he can pack in his cheeks,
And toucans and pecans and tin cans of sauce
And ham rolls and jam rolls and spindles of floss.
And he won't leave the table or push his chair back
Until he has asked for his eight o'clock snack,
And he'll find he can't button his extra-large shirt.

So if you see someone whose front side is bare
And it looks like his stomach's been pumped full of air,
You may cheer him along but stand back to cheer
For gluttons devour almost everything near.

For my part, I wouldn't dare be his server
For gluttons have eaten their nearby observers.
You can always tell gluttons – so be most alert,
For a glutton's a man who can't button his shirt.

## MARY ELIZABETH EVELYN MAY

"Mamma, where do babies come from?"
Asked Mary Elizabeth Evelyn May.
"They find them under cabbage leaves
Or pinkish bales of hay
And if you want to know anything more
I suggest you ask your father."

"Papa, where do babies come from?"
Asked Mary Elizabeth Evelyn May.
"They find them in bogs,
And mushrooms and logs,
And if you want to know anything more
I suggest you ask your brother."

"Bubba, where do babies come from?"
Asked Mary Elizabeth Evelyn May.
"They hatch from eggs of shredded cork
In steeple nests of giant storks.
And if you want to know anything more
I suggest you ask your doctor."

"Doctor, where do babies come from?"
Asked Mary Elizabeth Evelyn May.
"A hippo's sneeze or melon trees,
A matter of the birds and bees.
And if you want to know anything more
I suggest you ask your teacher."

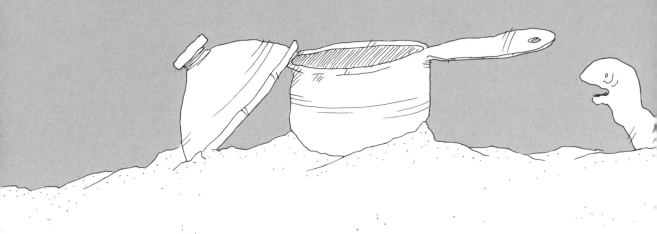

"Teacher, where do babies come from?"
Asked Mary Elizabeth Evelyn May.
"Well, not from trees and not from hay,
And not from birds and not from bees,
And not from watermelon seeds,
And not from bogs, or swamps, or logs,
And not from eggs and not from corks,
And not from sneezes or from storks,
And not from eating sugar cakes,
And not from reptile eggs or snakes.

"No matter what you may believe
They do not come from cabbage leaves.
I'm going to tell you straightaway
Mary Elizabeth Evelyn May
About how babies come to be."

And so she did
And Mary Elizabeth Evelyn May
Never will forget the day,
Her teacher helped her understand
Where babies do come from.

It's nice when grownups answer straight
It makes a kid feel pretty great!

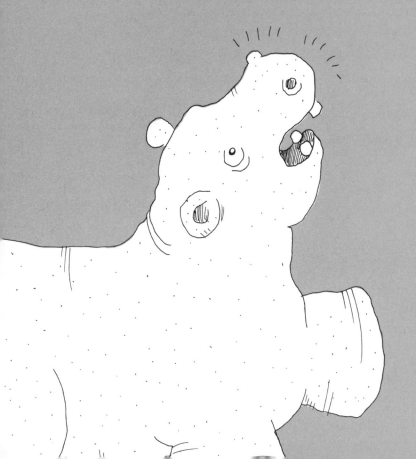

# JONAH'S PRAYER

When Jonah was swallowed by a fish . . .
Slosh, slosh, slurp, slurp!
He felt so foolish kneeling down
Slosh, slosh, slurp, slurp!
He prayed: "Help God, help . . . help!"
Slosh, slosh, slurp, slurp!
"If you can make a fish this big . . .
Surely you can make him burp!"

## NICE DOG

I met the nicest dog today.
I'm sure that he has fleas.
I tried to bring him in the house
And momma said "don't – please!
I'll bet that dog has ticks and fleas
And mites and mange and bugs."
She may be right, I cannot say,
I just know when I went to play
I met the nicest dog today.

## YOU CAN'T BUILD A STEEPLE
## THAT'S TALLER THAN GOD

The proud preacher, Dan, built a
Church and then planned
To build a tall steeple
That all of the people could see.
So . . .

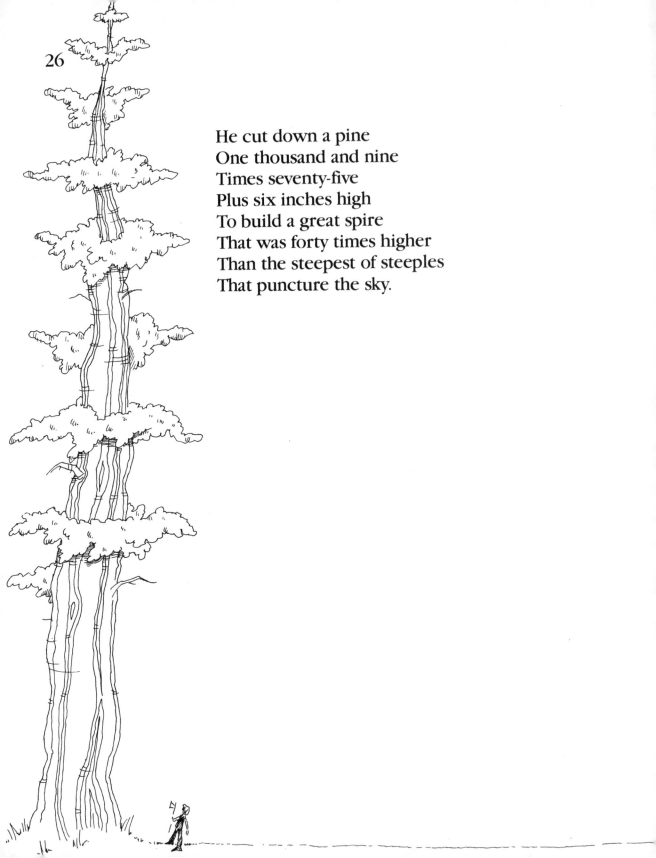

He cut down a pine
One thousand and nine
Times seventy-five
Plus six inches high
To build a great spire
That was forty times higher
Than the steepest of steeples
That puncture the sky.

"Why do you want
Such a very high steeple?"
Asked seven hundred and
Five thousand people.
"Because," said Dan,
"I want everyone to know
How stupendous I,
Reverend Dan, am.
I'll show them a church
They well can applaud
And build a great steeple
That's bigger than God!"

Then the sky clouded up
And a lightning bolt flashed
And a loud voice boomed
As the thunder crashed:
"This is God, Reverend Dan,
Now whatever you plan
Try to remember
I'm pretty good-sized
And if you should climb
From May to December,
You never could measure
How tall are the skies.
And even though all
In the whole world applaud
You can't build a steeple
That's bigger than God!"
God boomed and God thundered:
"See here, Reverend Dan,
Is a list of some things
That I'm taller than:

I'm taller than grass
I'm taller than flowers
Shrubs, poles, and trees
Chimneys and towers.
I'm taller than airplanes
Even jets in their flight.
I'm taller than rockets
That launch satellites.

It's too bad you've forgotten
(It's quite a disgrace)
For I'm taller than
Heaven and taller than space.
So you see, Pastor Dan,
You must tell the people
That I will always be
Taller than steeples."

But Dan didn't hear
The voice out of space.
He went out right then
To a very wide place
And started to build
At a very fast pace.
He found the great pine
One thousand and nine
Times seventy-five
Plus six inches high,
And he stood it on end
In a very strong wind
Till it disappeared
In the clouds of the sky.
"Oh, Reverend Dan,
That is a high steeple!"

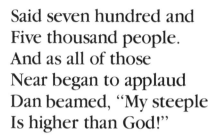

Said seven hundred and
Five thousand people.
And as all of those
Near began to applaud
Dan beamed, "My steeple
Is higher than God!"

And just as he spoke,
From the high clouds and mist
Came a thousand-mile hand
That formed in a fist.
It smashed the high steeple
Which fell all around
Shattered and scattered all over the ground.

Dan sat in the ruins
Of his tall splintered spire
Which no one around him
Now could admire.

He started to cry when the voice from the sky
Said, "Dan, I'm so sorry it ended this way.
But when life takes a turn
That helps us to learn.
We ought to admit it's been a good day."

No man is big who thinks he is big.
When we're uppity-up, we're only a clod.
We ought to remember we're made out of sod,
And we can't build a steeple
That's higher than God.

## PHONY PONY

If you see a horse with a beard and a horn
It could be you're seeing a real unicorn.
Or it could be some shyster has tied on a horn
To trick you to purchase a false unicorn.

You can be taken in and I think it is best
To make every horse pass the unicorn test.
Go slow and look closely when horses look weird.
Pull down on their horns and tug at their beards.
It's best to be sure about horses with horns.
Some ponies are phonies and not unicorns.

# FORMAL WEDDING

A great hippocerous and a rhinopotamus
Fell in love in an African swamp.
They were muddy and cruddy, but fully agreed
To be wed in the weeds and the reeds.

The guests who attended spoke words that were harsh.
They marveled that marriages made in a marsh
Were such murky affairs that the clean nearly cried
When they sang "Here comes the scum-covered bride."

While stuck in the muck, they both said "I do."
Inspired in the mire, they pledged to be true.
The music was brought by an African duck,
Who quacked out "Because" and "God Bless the Muck."

When the guests were all gone on the honeymoon night
The swamp had become a muck-lover's delight.
They plunged 'neath the mud and kissed in the muck
And wished each other the best kind of luck.

The hippocerous cooed, "My sweet rhinopotamus,
There's just you and I, but there's still quite a lot of us.
Our wedding was lovely, all formal with crud.
Oh, bliss that is ours to be stuck in the mud."

# TADDY AND POPSY

"You won't be a tadpole much longer my boy,"
Said the old Daddy frog in a slough.
"No matter how much you like tadding around
You'll be a bull frog when you're through!"
"Oh, please Father dear, I do like my tail!"
Said Tiny Tom Tad to his frog of a pop,
"I'd much rather fin with my finwiggle tail
Than have green spotted flippers that hop."

"But notice my Tiny Tom Tad of a pole
The little round bumps on the sides of your rump,
They will certainly sprout as you swim all about
Some hoppity legs that go thumpety thump."

"Never," cried Tom, as he swam in the pond
Making little round "o's" with his "o" of a mouth.
But before very long as he swam to the north
He felt some new legs trailing back to the south.
"Your finwiggle tail is eroding, Tad Tommy,"
Said the doughty old frog to his green-legged tad.
Those bumps aren't just mumps that you see on your neck.
You'll soon sprout front legs and look just like your dad."
"I won't be a bull frog!" said the tad to his daddy,
"Frog-hoppers aren't proper."
He left for a day and when he returned
His front legs had sprouted: his tail gone away.
He tried to make "o's" but his "o's" wouldn't come.
He looked for his tail feeling terribly dumb.

He looked all around the green mossy bog
At his front legs and back legs, then climbed on a log.
"Frog Popsy, Frog Popsy"; he croaked through the fog,
"Popsy, it's Taddy, I think I'm a frog!
But froghood's not bad
Oh, what a surprise!
There's so much to do in this marvelous slough.
Teach me to hop and snag dragonflies."
As Taddy became a croak-happy hopper
He knew he would never make "o's" again, never!
"You're a bull of a frog," said his frog of a pop,
"It's right to feel proud and so green-spotted clever.
Froghood is rough, but you had to grow up,
'Cause you can't stay a tadpole forever."

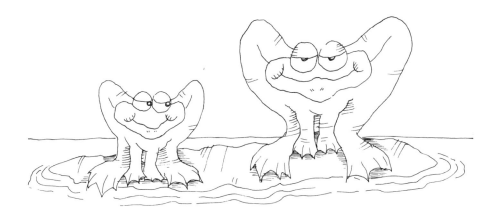

## I'M GONNA HAVE A BABY, ABIE!

Haven't you found that the mothers you know
Quit having babies at forty or so.
But Sarah at eighty though wrinkled and gray
Sat knitting booties through most of the day.
When Abraham said to her, "Sarah you're knitting,
I feel that it's fitting that you tell me why."
Old Sarah just winked, then smiled and replied,
"I'm going to have a baby, Abie."

It sounded so funny, they giggled out loud,
They bellowed and laughed and attracted a crowd
Who asked Abraham:
"What is so funny – could you tell us, maybe?"
"My Sarah is eighty, expecting a baby!"

"A baby! A baby!" They shouted with glee!
They rollicked and frolicked hilariously,
Holding their sides and slapping their knees!
They fell on the ground and roared out with joy,
"Tell us, old Sarah – a girl or a boy?"

When one of them saw she was knitting some booties
They broke out in laughing and roaring and hooting.
One of them mocked her: "She's quite off her rocker!
Dear Lady, you're eighty, you can't have a baby!

They hooted and howled; for nine months they roared.
They made so much noise that they nearly ignored
The sound of the postman who knocked at the door,
"Hey fellas! A letter from Abie has come.
Old Sarah his wife had a new little son!"
At last they quit laughing,
And yet they felt joy,
And all ran to Abie's
To see his new boy.
They all smiled at Abie and said "Happy Baby!"
While Abraham beamed as proud as could be.
But God smiled down on nobody other
Than Sarah, the old one, the happy new mother!

## DANIEL'S PRAYER

Oh, God
I promise to obey your law
If all these kitties get lockjaw.

Please God, I'm frankly scared to death!
Don't let these cats get prophet's breath.

                              Amen.

# OVERBITE AND CHEAP COLOGNE

"Roberta Beaver!" Said Samantha Skunk,
"Your upper teeth protrude the longest!
Your overbite is molar white.
You must, dear, please, quit gnawing trees
And see your orthodontist."

"Samantha Skunk!" Said Roberta Beaver,
"How dare you criticize! Your odor is well known!
It's not polite
To talk about my overbite!
Where do you buy such rank cologne?"

## FLOSSIE FLEA AND
## THE GREEN SAINT BERNARD

When Flossie Flea chose a home for herself
She chose a green Saint Bernard
And she told all her friends
Who had picked smaller dogs,
"I wanted a dog with a yard!"

But as Flossie grew older, she had second thoughts.
She saw her huge home like a critic.
She had varicose veins in her short stubby wings
And her six knotted legs were arthritic.

In her ninetieth year as fleas reckon years
Her excitement at leaving her Saint Bernard grew.
It happened one day on the thirteenth of May
That she spotted a shaggy, bright green peek-a-poo!

"It takes me a year on this great Saint Bernard
To walk from his head to his tail and return.
I'm moving this week to this poo-of-a-peek
And retire where the fur is much greener."

So she left her green Saint, flew over the gate
And landed astride the green peek-a-poo!
"I'm happy at last to be free of the past,
I'll never leave peekie, whatever I do."

In three pairs of tennies she set out to walk
Exploring her peekie with joy.
But she found out quite soon that well before noon
She could walk tiny laps to his collar and back.
She thought that the trip would be some sort of test
But she did it without even stopping to rest.
It was then she discovered she'd made a mistake
For the green peek-a-poo was confining.
"I don't like this poo, I know what I'll do,
I'm moving right back to my green Saint Bernard."

"At last now I know that wherever I go
I will always enjoy my green Saint Bernard.
My wisdom is keener: the fur just looks greener
On the plush woolly dog in the neighbor's back yard."

## WHITE TRUCK

I always thought that I would be
A fireman on a big red truck.
But Mr. Garibaldi comes every Saturday.
He only comes to pick up trash
And haul it all away
And yet he always talks to me
Before he dumps the can.

He's been so very nice
That when I become a man
I'd like to get a big white truck
And drive down every street
And stop at every garbage can
To see who I might meet.

## JONATHAN HERRINGTON BARRINGTON GREEN

"You can't get down 'til you've finished your beans,
Jonathan Herrington Barrington Green!
It just isn't right to eat what you please
Seventeen helpings of 'roni and cheese,
One half a pie and a strawberry freeze
And not finish one little helping of beans!"
On the thirteenth of May, [ninety two seventeen]
Jonathan Herrington Barrington Green
Looked at his plate of uneaten beans
And said to his mother, Gladys Maureen,
"I won't eat these veggies. I hate these green beans!"
"Then you'll never get down," said his mother.
So he sat there all day and looked far away,
And all through the night 'til the fourteenth of May.
"May I get down now, Mother, sweet Gladys Maureen?"
"Jonathan Herrington Barrington Green, are you sure you have
    eaten every last bean?"
"No!" said the boy.
"No!" said his mother.
And so passed away
The fourteenth of May.

Jonathan sat with his chin stuck way out
For a month and a day and a day and a month,
'Til the summer was gone and autumn had come,
And a day and a month and a month and a day
'Til skies became gray and the snow fell around
And settled upon his old plate of beans.
"Oh, Mother, dear Mother, sweet Gladys Maureen,
It's snowing all over my plate of green beans.
Please may I get down from this table and go,
For I hate my green beans when they're cold as the snow."
"No, not 'til you've finished every last bean!"

Another year passed, then twenty-one more
And Jonathan's mother was now eighty-four
And the beans didn't look so good anymore.
"Please, Mother, these beans are too old – May I go?"
His mother was aged but firmly said, "No!"
Jonathan Green never left home again.
He never played football or made a new friend.
He nevermore studied or traveled or wed.
For fifty-five years he never ate bread
He never slept in a fluffy soft bed.
In his ninetieth year when his beard had grown long
He choked down the beans by the light of the moon.
"Mmm! These weren't so bad!" said Jonathan Green,
"I wish now I'd listened to Gladys Maureen."

# CATHERINE CATERPILLAR

Mother caterpillar turned to her daughter one day
And said, "My sweet Catherine, I'm going away
And I cannot come back – I'm sorry to say."

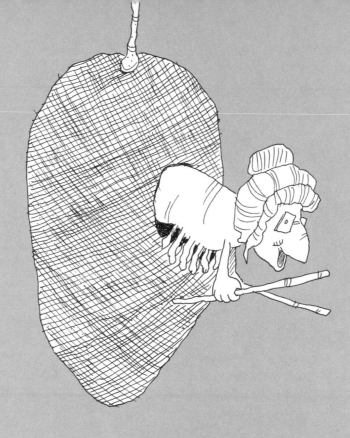

She clipped the last threads on her bright new cocoon
And then turned to Catherine again,
"Well, Cathy, I'm going in now –
Are you sure you quite understand,
Can you spin the webbing and knit the silk threads
And fleece the insides of your own little pod?"
"Yes, Mother, I can," said Catherine Caterpillar.

"I've woven the uprights, just as you said
And tied off three hundred and seventy threads.
I am sure that before the birth of the moon
I'll be more than prepared for my own cocoon."
They kissed goodbye on a dried milk-pod twig
And the old woolly worm adjusted her wig
And crawled on into her vacant cocoon.
Catherine was scared, "Is it true I will lose all my legs . . ."
"Yes, Catherine, almost – you get to keep six."
"Only six – oh, what then?"
Her mother knitted the last thirty threads
And answered her from her own downy bed.
"Catherine, you'll never walk, ever again!"
She pulled the last threads and closed her cocoon and was gone.

Cathy spent thirteen days weaving and webbing,
Packing in fleece and cutting the threads.
When the day at last came to enter her pod,
Catherine looked sadly down at her two hundred legs
And spoke very sharply to God:

"God, this is Catherine Caterpillar
I don't mean to gripe, but you haven't been fair,
And I haven't got long now to talk.
Already I feel a frost in the air.
But God, it's like this, I've two hundred legs
And while it's an effort to climb up a stalk,
I enjoy so much just crawling along
and taking a nice autumn walk.
Please God, if you don't mind, could I keep my legs?"
But God only smiled and pulled out the moon
While Catherine looked down at her two-hundred legs
And stomped her way into her fleecy cocoon.
For a hundred and seventy days the frost gathered.
God smiled as snowflakes piled high on the thread
And Catherine slept warm in her soft fleecy bed.

And seven cold moons smiled down on the snow
'Til in May God came rapping on Catherine's cocoon.
"It's terribly dark," said Catherine in fright,
"I must clip these threads and let in some light."

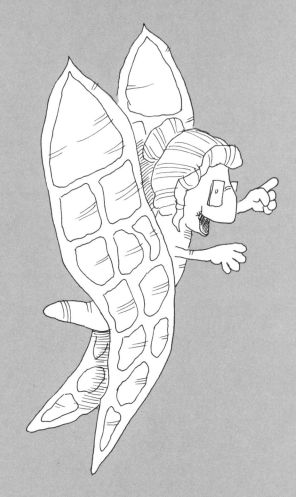

She chewed through the webbing and cut the silk threads
And crawled out and stretched, then suddenly thought
As she looked at her bed,
"My legs are gone . . . Oh, what will I do? I cannot go far."

She looked and saw a winged creature who
Landed in splendor on the old milkpod twig.
"Catherine Caterpillar, the morning is bright!"
"Mother, it's you! I've lost all my legs, I think
I will die."
"Nonsense; you're at the beginning of life –
You're not going to die.
You're through crawling, dear Catherine, look up at
The Sky!
When God takes our legs he expects us to fly."

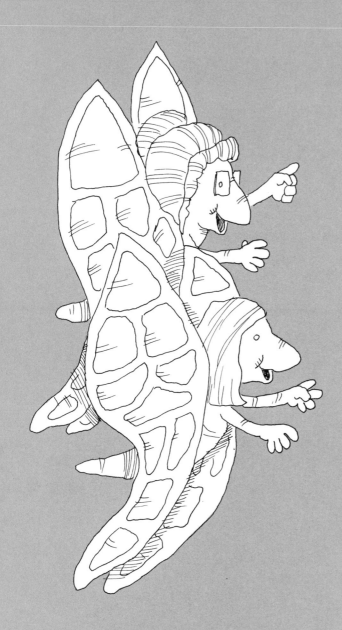

Catherine looked back at the weathered cocoon and
Tried her new wings, they both rose and flew.
"I never knew, Mother, that skies were so blue,"
"Stretch out your wings and float on the wind
And tell me, do you want to be what you've been,
And crawl in the dust and have legs once again."
"Oh Mother, I'm flying! Today all is sky!
And surely God's watching as we flutter by.
He watches the winters and guards the cocoons
And smiles while the snow falls beneath icy moons.
He laughs at our fears while the winter wind sings,
And wakes us to fly on filagreed wings."

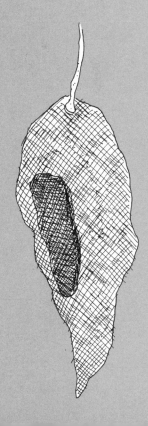

## IT DOESN'T HELP TO HELP A CHICK

You can't help a chick
To hatch from an egg,
'Cause the shell
Sometimes sticks
To his head or his leg
And he'll cheep
And he'll yell
For when you pick his shell
You'll really be pulling his leg.
No matter how much we'd all like to help
There's some things a chick must do for himself.

# EAT THE EYE FIRST

Whenever I'm served
A whole fish with a head
And its fried eye
Glares up from the table,
I eat the eye first
So the fish cannot watch
While I eat
The rest (if I'm able).

So if you're served a fish
That gawks from its dish
As its fishy eye stares
And makes you feel cursed,
You'll enjoy it more
If you eat the eye first.

# DAVID AND GOLIATH

Goliath: Fee, Fie, Fo,
        Foy
        I smell the blood
        of a little boy!

David: Don't mind me,
        Goliath, I'm
        Just collecting
        rocks.

Goliath: Fee, Fie, Fo,
        Feek!
        Little shepherd
        boys are weak!

David: Don't be too sure.
Oh, look, I found another
rock.

Goliath: Fee, Fie, Fo, Foff!
I'm gonna knock
your head clear off!

David: One more rock,
that makes three.
And here's one more and
that makes four . . .
Here's another, sakes
alive . . . now there's
five.

Goliath: Fee, Fie, Fo, Fot
Whether you got rocks
or not
I'll get you, you
slingshot tot.

David: Ready or not
Here comes a rock!

Goliath: Fee, Fie, Fo, Fed
What's this sticking in
my head?
Oops! I'm dead!

## HALVERSON HAWK

Halverson Hawk
Could swoop from the skies and
Land on a rat
And gobble him up and then broadly
Smile

And all of the while feeling wonderful
That
He was freeing the world of hundreds of rats.

But one sunny day Halverson Hawk
Folded his wings and went for a walk
And peeked in a rat hole and saw Mrs. Rat
Who was holding her sick little ratling named Mike,
A ratty and lovable, sick little tyke.

Halverson tilted his hawk ears to hear
Mrs. Rat praying and weeping in fear,
"Oh, God of all rats,
We rats aren't well off –
The hawks all about us won't give us a nod,
They swoop from the skies and gobble us, God.
Now I'm not complaining, but just for a spell
You made little Mikey, please make him get well."

A rat tear crossed her furry gray nose
And Halverson Hawk stretched and then rose,
He soared and then spun away high in the blue
Where something in Halverson seemed born anew.

He couldn't help thinking of Mrs. Rat's prayer.
He could still see her tears as he flew through the air,
He would never forget how sadly she sat
Asking the rat god to care for her rat.
And each time he swooped or dived at another
He felt more and more that each rat was his brother,
And the rattiest rat was a joy to his mother.

## YOU CAN'T TAKE A PLANT FOR A WALK

If you live alone and don't want to be lonely
You should buy yourself a puppy or plant.
A fluffy, soft puppy is better because
A puppy can walk but a plant simply can't.

You can't put a plant on a leash for a walk,
But plants are good listeners whenever you talk.
You can tell them your problems and plants never mock,
While you dibble their roots and prop up their stalks.
You can wrap them in blankets and set them on rocks
And use their small branches to hang up your socks.
You can let them make friends with a grandfather clock
Or replant them each day in shiny new crocks.
I suppose you could dress them in long formal frocks,

Though some of your friends might marvel and gawk
And those who hate house plants might gossip and talk.
But never forget that for all of your toil
You must leave a plant with its feet in the soil.
So, if you'd like a friend to wander and walk
And skip along lanes and hop over rocks,
Plants are good listeners whenever you talk
But puppies are better than leaves on a stalk,
'Cause plants only stand with their roots tied in knots.
They can't take one step from their safe little pots.
Believe me, you can't take a plant for a walk.

## WORMS

Nobody likes being called a mere worm,
Though I cannot understand why.
Worms never swear and worms never yell,
And worms never ever tell lies.
Worms rarely feel blue or look downcast, it's true.
Have you ever seen a worm cry?
They live in the earth but they're never depressed.
They crawl but they never get dirt in their eyes.
They cannot stand up, so they never fall down,
And you cannot bury a worm in the ground.
Worms never bite and worms will not fight.
Worms never shout or wake you at night.
Worms are wiggly and wet and wonderfully true,
Still, who wants to be one? I don't, do you?

## KISSING ALL THE
## UGLY OUT

In an enchanted forest
A beautiful young toad
Discovered a Prince,
Beside a dark road.

"I do need a husband
To share my small home
I'll just kiss this prince
So I won't be alone.

"Still I must try to keep
My kiss very short
For people can cause
A toad to grow warts!"

The man seemed so ugly
She didn't dare peek
As she kissed the drab Prince
Right on his cheek.

The Prince then became
A strong handsome toad,
And they married right there
Beside the dark road,
And there in a puddle
Surrounded by heather
Raised thousands of tadpoles
And were happy together.

If you sometimes feel lonely
Use good common sense.
There's a handsome toad
Hiding in some ugly Prince.
Kiss each one you see
And do it with cheer,
Hug hugely, love bravely,
And kiss without fear.

## MARIONETTA

Marionetta wanted to be a real girl.
She was always on stage where she'd dance and she'd sing
But when everyone left the theater at night
Marionetta was stranded, still tied to her strings.
Her strings were five and they kept her alive,
One for each hand and one for each foot
And for the top of her head.

The other string dancers had warned her so often
That without her five strings she'd be dead,

But Marionetta would hang in the dark
When all of the children were gone,
She'd cry ever softly and wish for the light
And dream of a day without strings.

Then she'd be free to run down a walk
Or skate like a demon through wide parking lots.
She'd run through a meadow and chase butterflies,
Climb trees without getting all tangled in knots.
She'd fly from her shadows and dance on the wind
And listen to locusts and katydids sing,
And she would be free as a robin or a swallow,
With never the tug or the yank of a string.

One night after acting she hung on a board
Her dark strings were knotted and twisted in cords.
"Marionetta," a kind voice spoke in the dark,
"Would you come with me to the mountains and sea
If I cut your strings so you could be free?"

"Yes, yes," she cried, "but I'm knotted in cords.
I'm hanging quite backwards and facing the boards."
"I'm the master of dancers, I'll cut all your strings
You'll dance in the light where the katydid sings."

The other string dancers began to object,
"Don't trust him, you'll die. He promises things
But our kind can't live or move without strings."
"I'd rather be dead than tied up in cords
All knotted in darkness and facing the boards,
Come, master of dancers, and cut off these strings."

In the dark Marionetta could not see a thing
As the string dancers' master drew near.
But she heard a brief snip and felt a string clipped
And her left leg fell free and dangled in air.

A second snip came and she hung splendidly
And two more short snips and her hands dangled free.
She hung by one string on the top of her head.
With one final snip she tumbled like lead
And the string dancers cried, "The poor girl is dead."

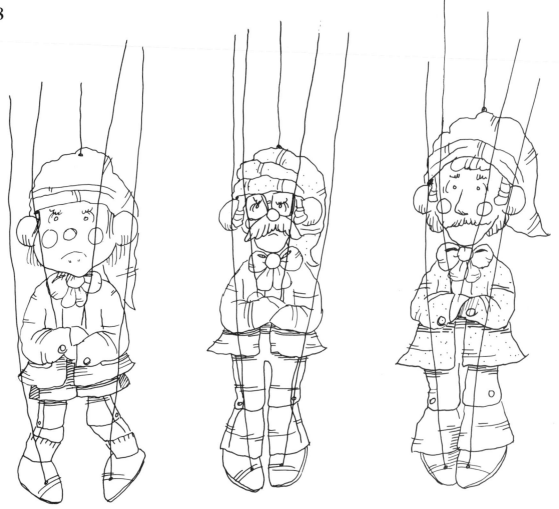

"Oh no, I'm not," said a voice in the dark,
"I'm free of the strings and I'll follow the lark."
When the morning light came on the edge of the dawn
Everyone saw Marionetta was gone.
They doubted the voice that had called in the night,
That promised the dancer a life in the light.
They hung in their cords, the poor knotted things,
Insisting that no one could live without strings.

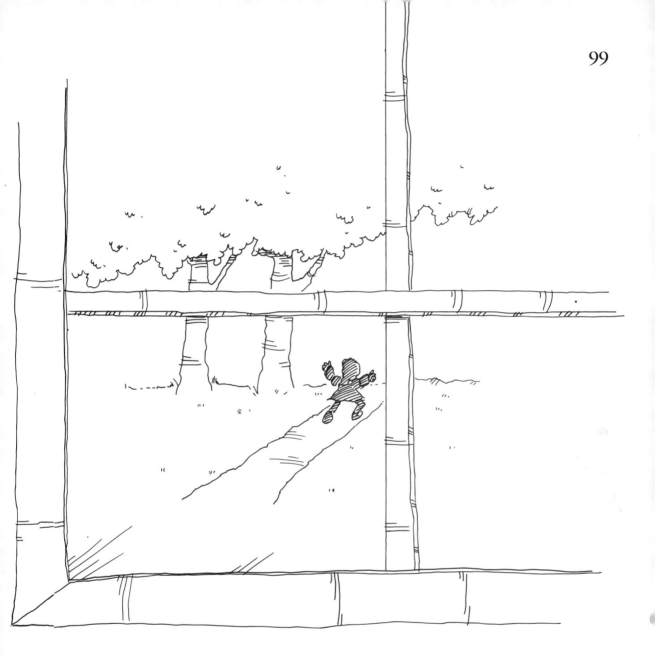

But Marionetta knew sunshine and joy
And ran through the meadows where katydids sing.
She chased her fast shadow where waterfalls spring,
So glad she had chosen a life without strings.

# THIN-SHELLED CONCEIT

Humpty-Dumpty was calcium plumpsy
And thin-brittle-proud, a real egg of a bloke!
He was only a cell, a yellow-souled shell
All mushable, crushable egg-white and yolk.
He wanted to be a high-flying egg
And frolic on walls where eggs rarely ambled
And it takes some conceit for an egg on two feet
To climb on a wall, all mossy and brambled.
Up on the high wall he tottered and tumbled
Then skipped, slipped, and plunged, and he ended up scrambled.

Near the base of the wall where Humpty has fallen
There now stands a marker – an egg on a column –
The words cut in marble say simply and solemn,
"Things sure do get messy
All yellow and fizz,
When a smart-aleck egg
Forgets who he is!"

## JOSEPH'S CHARTREUSE/FUCHSIA
## BLAZER

Some men have twelve sons
But only see one.
Joseph's Daddy, Jacob,
Gave him a wild new
Chartreuse, blue
Fuchsia,
Hot-pink blazer.
It glowed like an electric cherry,
A glittering supercharged
Rainbow of light.
Its collar was made of
Lightning bright lasers.
His coat was truly a high-voltage blazer.

Joseph's plain brothers were very upset,
Because their dad, Jacob, made Joseph his pet.
Yes, Judah, Issachar, Reuben, and Dan
And Asher and Levi were mad to a man.
"Its bad," said Gad, "that Jacob, our dad,
Treats Joseph as though
He's the one son he's had."

"I'm wearing a jacket, an old hand-me-down,
It's soiled and dirty and ragged and torn,"
Said Judah, "I had it when Joseph was born.
I've patched it six times and the zipper is broken.
What can Dad mean giving Joseph this coat?"

Then Joseph came by in his video cloak
Which glowed in the dark like a star.
"Look fellows, you're jealous, just try to admit
My garment's refractive
Like radioactive.
A jolt of a coat, an electric grid weave.
I'm a live neon leon
In a hot double-breaster
With high amperage sleeves."

"Enough is enough," said Reuben, the rough.
The story goes badly I'm sorry to tell.
Joseph the proud, wound up in a well.
Slavery was his lot, with no coat of his own.
His old grieving father felt very alone.

The brothers were selfish – still you should take note
That if ever you're given a high voltage coat
Don't flaunt it at those who have barely a stitch
When everyone's wearing a cheap threadbare coat
You're smart to avoid a high-voltage gloat.

## BLUEBERRY TERRY

"Sweet Strawberry Sherry, will you ever marry?"
Asked Blueberry Terry, but she shook her head.
"I find marriage scary, dear Blueberry Terry,
Ask Razberry Mary to marry instead."

"I'll not marry Terry," said Razberry Mary, "for Blueberry Terry
Resides on the prairie: I won't leave my dairy to follow him
West."
"Then you I can't marry," said Blueberry Terry – "I won't
Leave the prairie to work for a dairy – dear Strawberry Sherry,
Please marry me now.

"No, Terry, like Mary, I do not like prairie.
I live on a ferry and never would marry
A man so content to care for his cows."

"Very well, Sherry.
Very well, Mary.
I'll leave the prairie,
Will one of you marry
Me now?"

"I don't find you handsome," said Razberry Mary.

"I don't find you wealthy," said Strawberry Sherry.

"And since you're not handsome and do not have wealth,
We think that we'll soon marry somebody else."
So Blueberry Terry returned to the prairie and
Rarely saw Mary and Sherry, but then
Mary and Sherry at their ferry and dairy never
Were asked if they'd marry again.

At the dairy and ferry they grew old and thin.
They were all nearly ninety when they hobbled in,
"Dear Blueberry Terry," said Strawberry Sherry, "I've
Changed my mind Terry, I'll marry you now."
"Yes Terry, Dear Terry," said Razberry Mary, "I'll
Marry you Terry, I'll marry and how!"

"I don't find you pretty, I don't find you healthy
And since you are ugly and have no real wealth
I think I'll return to my cows and my prairie
And there I may marry somebody else."

"I don't really know who I'll marry now,
I'm living alone surrounded by cows."

In a small cemetery they buried old Mary and
Poor lonely Sherry, whose tombstones there read:
"Here Strawberry Sherry and Razberry Mary
were buried, unmarried – both single and dead."
Old Blueberry Terry – their man from the prairie –
Felt so alone as his final years sped
He married his Guernsey far out in the prairie
Delighted he'd finally found something to wed.

## TWENTY-FIVE CENTS

Save a thousand thousand dollars
And you'll be a millionaire,
Save a thousand million dollars
And you'll be a billionaire.

But if you only save a quarter
You can buy a party hat
And put it on and sing a song,
And stand and cheer and laugh.

Or with a quarter's worth of foil
You can shape a shining crown
And make yourself a gallant king
In just a dressing gown.

For one quarter buy a stick
And make it be a cracking whip
And get yourself a cane and chair,
And make-believe lions
With great shaggy manes
Will leap and soar
Through hoops of flame.
If you only have a quarter
You can live with dash and flair
As a king or lion trainer
When you're just a "quarter-aire."

# NEEDLES

Needles Potts
Loved to give shots,
With a long square needle
And a two-quart syringe.
Above the knee-joint
He would jab in the point
And laughing in vigor
He'd squeeze on the trigger
While the patients he treated
Would whimper and cringe.

He'd often give babies
Shots to cure rabies
Though babies with rabies
Are really quite rare.
He'd simply say
Maybe this baby has rabies
I'd better just wheedle
My needle in here.

If he saw a rabbit
He'd jab it and stare.
He called this cruel habit
The shooting of hares.

He'd vaccinate llamas
And rhinos and Brahmas
And hippos and gators
And grown pachyderms.

He'd stick his steel point
In a hummingbird's joint
For he claimed that the birds
Were humming with germs.
And laughing hyenas
Seeing his needle,

Stopped their laughing
And cried in alarm.
He loved octopi
And when one happened by
He would vaccinate eight times –
A shot in each arm.

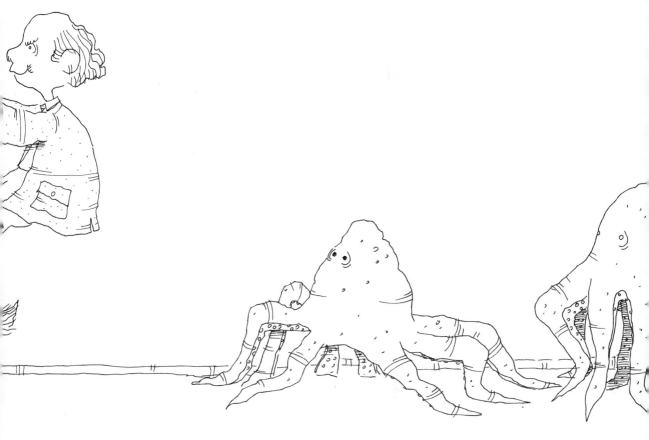

But most of his pleasure
Came from the children.
He'd stick in his needle
And laugh through the day.
He'd stick it in fast and
Twist it and laugh.
Some places he'd put it
We really can't say.
He'd stick it in knees

And elbows and toes
And leg bones and fingers.
Eyebrows near eyes,
(While kiddies all cried),
And triceps and biceps
And molars and shoulders,
And tonsils and thighs.

One day it happened,
Needles Potts became ill.
He went to a doctor
Who studied him well
And said very gravely
"My dear Needles Potts,
You have a condition
That cannot be cured.
My poor Dr. Potts
This sad word I give,
You must have every day
Some thirty-two shots,
Yes, thirty-two shots
For as long as you live.
Your case, Dr. Potts,
Is most horrid, I fear,
Thirty-two daily,
Have I made myself clear?
That's eleven thousand
And more shots a year."

He started to cry.
His doctor said, "Needles,
You're crying, but why?
I thought you liked shots."
"I hate shots," said Potts.
"Shots are no fun
If I get the stabbing,
They only bring joy
When I do the jabbing."

There ever after
The good Dr. Potts
Got thousands and thousands
And thousands of shots.
He was shot full of holes
As he walked around town
The holiest doctor around.

So if you like causing anyone pain
Remember his story again and again.
Be gentle and kind and ever alert
Never to laugh when anyone hurts,
And then ask yourself,
"Just what would you do
If the hurt of another
Was given to you."
Remember the fate
Of poor Needles Potts
Who as far as I know
Still suffers lots
Getting thousands and thousands
And thousands of shots.

# JACK SPRAT

Jack Sprat can eat no fat
And Mrs. Sprat (who's very fat)
Is glad of that!

## THE TWENTY-DAY SERMON

The twenty-day sermon
Of Reverend Tom Herman
Began on a Sunday
And lasted three weeks.
And nobody stayed
Till the sermon was done.
When God came to town
The Reverend Tom Herman
Invited God over
To hear Herman speak,
But God replied, "Tom,
I can't stay that long
I'm only in town for the week."

## PHARAOH'S GALOSHES

One day when Moses was tending his sheep
And stood leaning on his rod,
He saw a juniper bush ablaze.
"Land o'Goshen!" Moses gasped.
"Funny you should bring that up!" said God.

"In the land of Goshen, not too far from the Pyramids
A Pharaoh rules called Big Ramses.
My people are slaves to his demands."
"Well that beats all," Moses replied.
"Funny you should bring that up; listen please!"

"He does beat them all – yes every one
He beats them every day," said God.
"Moses, would you set them free?"
"My goodness, God," Moses allowed,
"They must add up to an awful crowd!"

"Funny you should bring that up, Moses,
There's really quite a few.
But I figured you could get them through
The deserts, swamps, and seas,
So I chose you."

"Great balls of fire," gasped Moses.
"Funny you should bring that up,
Here's what I'll do.
By night, I'll give you balls of fire
So you'll have light to lead them through!"
"Flippin' fleas," Moses cried.
"Of course," said God,
"You go and tell King Ramses
That Egypt will be scratchin' fleas
Until he lets them go."

So Moses went down to Egypt
And walked right up to Pharaoh's door
And knocked, and Pharaoh opened up!

"Now look Ramses – you're the big cheese
And God always starts at the top.
Those slaves down in Goshen are raking in dough,
They're making you rich, but God wants you to stop.
I'm telling you, 'Ramsey,' you better lay low
'Cause these folk are God's
And He says, 'Let 'em go!'"

Well, God sent the fleas,
Downtown and suburban
And 'Ramsey' found bugs in his
Toga and turban.
There were bugs in his figs,
Cheese, mattress, and
Showers.
There were bugs in his
Biscuits and dungeon
And towers.
"Quit buggin' me God! Quit
Buggin' me please!"
"I'm glad you brought that up
Ramses.
Will you let my people go?"
"Anything! Anything! Just promise me
Please,
That I can quit scratching and digging at fleas."

I'll shorten this tale, but may I still say
That God bugged old 'Ramsey' ten different ways
'Til properly bugged he set the slaves free
And they stood with the fireballs beside the Red Sea.

But then Pharaoh came with ten thousand men
"I've changed my mind, Moses," he said with a grin.
"I want all of you home, both women and men.
I own you, you're mine! You're slaves once again!
And if you won't come back to Egypt with me
I'll finish you off here beside the Red Sea."
"Great walls of water!" cried Moses.

"I'm glad you brought that up," said God.
"Just look at the sea and stick out your rod."
So Moses did.
The sea parted in two and a nation of slaves
Passed right on through,
And Ramsey's men followed, but soon were aghast.
For the high walls of water through which his men passed
Tilted and buckled then leaned and collapsed.

"My soldiers are drowned in the depths of the sea!"
Old Pharaoh cried out as he fell to his knees.
"Oh, how I wish I had listened to God.
Alas, goodness me, and thirty two goshes!
My army is lost where the sea water washes,
While I stand here helpless in muddy galoshes."

## FOUR IN THE FLOOR

"Here's my furnace, in you go
Shadrach, Meshach, and Abednego.
I told you before
You should have bowed low
To this big golden idol of mine.
I'll roast you slow
To a golden brown
And anyone else
In Babylon town
Who refuses
To worship my idol."
Said Nebuchadnezzar,
"It gives me great pleasure
To throw you all
Into the hot, hot fire."

But Shadrach and Meshach weren't even singed.
They just talked low to Abednego,
While the flames all blazed and the furnace roared
Into the fire came their fireproof Lord.
"Look, Nebuchadnezzar, would you please, sir!"
Cried Shadrach, Meshach and Abednego.
"We all plan to stick together
And we'd like you to know, Mr. Nebuchadnezzar,
That God is our friend and He is so trustable
He has made each one of us noncombustible.
You threw in three but the fire won't burn us
'Cause there's four in the floor of your fiery furnace."

## WHEN THE AARDVARK
## PARKED ON THE ARK
## IN THE DARK

The night was black
As a midnight storm
And the rain fell wet and cold.
The deepness of night
Was as dark as a pit
And a thousand animals
Howled and growled
And shrieked and roared.

The flood was coming,
But hadn't begun
When the animals
Climbed the ramp.
They barked in the dark
They trumpeted and hooted,
And cried as they came aboard.

In the dark and the damp
At the top of the ramp
Two elephants fell
On two kangaroos.
The startled hyenas
Laughed high piercing laughs
Which frightened two zebras
Which scared the giraffes.

They kicked over the warthogs
Who scared the panda bears
Who roared at the lions
And tigers and bison
.Who trampled the badgers
And raccoons and coneys.

They ran under the camels
And Clydesdales and ponies
Till the jerseys and holsteins
And guernseys went "moo"
And the hippos went "hip"
And the rhinos all "rhined."

The orangutans screamed!
Then the lightning bugs shined.
And the glowworms took courage
And faced the brave night
Til Noah switched on
The neon-sign eels
And lit up the ark
With electric-eel light.
It was suddenly clear
What went wrong in the night.

For there on the ark
At the top of the stairs
The aardvarks looked very
Ashamed and quite humble
For they had caused
The elephants to stumble.
And this clearly proves
That if you are leading
And the line that you lead
Is quite in the dark
You must not stop walking
For those just behind
Could trip over you and be hard to find.
If you want to help out
As you live out your life
And help other people
Find joy day by day,
Either follow or lead
And if neither of these
Be sure you keep out of the way.

## "I-NESS"

I'm me, and my "I-ness" is special to me.
Minus my "I-ness" I'd just be like you,
And you'd be like me and that's nothing new.
"You-ness" looks good, but only on you.
'Cause "you-ness" won't fit where "I-ness" should be.
My "I-ness" looks great, but only on me.

# CONCEITED

Rah rah, rah rah rah!
Rah rah, rah rah rah!
Rah rah, rah rah rah!
MOI!

## SNOW-FOLK

I made a giant snowman,
He was three balls tall
With charcoal eyes
And a stovepipe hat
But all alone in the yard,
So,

I made a giant snow-wife,
She too was three balls tall,
(Though the balls were small).
She had a six-coal-chunk smile,
But even as she leaned
On the kitchen broom
I could tell
The both of them were
Childless and unhappy
So,

I made five little snow-kids,
Each just two balls tall,
They didn't mind,
Like all snow-tots
They fussed and fought
In the new cold snow
Then they laid down
And dreamed of a magic day ahead.

They called their snow-folks
Jean and Fred.
Still the snow-kids looked so lonely
All through the winter day,
I knew they needed other friends
So they could run and play,
So,

I made sixteen brand-new snow-friends,
Wow, what a time they had!
They played white games
And danced and laughed
And sang as the sun rolled out.

They would be happy yet, I know
But they thawed and cried
As they grew wet.
Nothing lasts forever
But I won't forget the day
That Fred and Jean and their five tots
Had the snow-friends in to play.

# THIN MINNY

"I'm simply too fat!" cried Minny McBride
When she found herself stuck in a slippery slide.
And there halfway down she wailed and she cried.
"I must lose some weight, I've grown far too wide.
I'm embarrassed to find myself wedged in this slide.
I'm giving up chocolates," wept Minny McBride,
"Spaghetti and bonbons and everything fried."

Six firemen came, they pushed and they pried,
Until they popped Minny right out of that slide.
She then lost some weight and regained her pride
But she went overboard with her calorie guide.

So Minny grew skinny – just three inches wide.
And the first gust of wind
Blew her back up the slide.

## THE WORMS' FRIENDLY GREETING

Do you know how earthworms shake hands
When they meet in their worm holes under the land?
They twine their thin bodies and circle each other
And say, "Hello, friend, and how is your mother?"
We could learn a lot from worms
To make our handshakes good and firm.

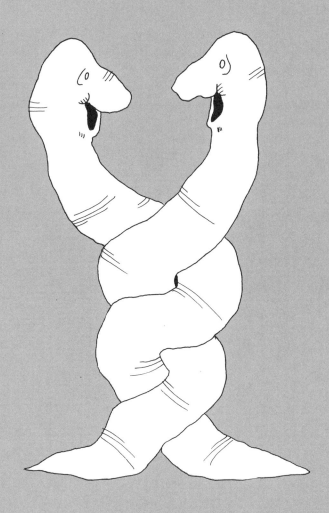

## FREE VERSE

One, two, shut the door,
Three, four, button your shoe,
Five, six, big fat hen,
Seven, eight, pick up sticks,
Nine, ten, close the gate.
It's hard to learn to count to ten,
If you don't know what rhymes with "hen."

## HERMIONE WHITE

"I'm Hermione White of Whittington Abbey,"
Said the elegant pigeon to Sue Ellen Swallow.

"I've a nest in the church west of the Thames –
It's a poor little church with a small white steeple,
And attended, I fear, by the poorest of people,"
Said Sue Ellen Swallow.

Hermione White was refined and angelic,
All feathered snow and pure as a dove.
She usually fluttered above the high towers
And cooed out her high-flying, formal, white hymns.
Sue Ellen Swallow felt crumpled and ruffled,
Ashamed of her nest in the small wooden church by the
Thames.
"What's it like, Hermione, high in the tower above the
Bronze bells when you're talking to God?"

"My dear little swallow, you must come and see.
You can always see God on shiny clear days."
"Have you seen Him yourself?" asked Sue Ellen Swallow.
"Oh, yes, my poor child – I meet Him up there,"
She pointed her broad wing into the air.
"He's all white, Sue Ellen, much like myself,"
Hermione gushed.
"You say you live in a wooden frame church . . . it must be
Quite hard to see Him from there . . .
The steeple's so low, the building's so shabby.
I worship the high and lofty white God
Who rules over all from Whittington Abbey."

"I must get back to my swallowlings now."
"How many are there?" Hermione asked.
"Ten," said Sue Ellen, looking away.
"Ten!" gasped the pigeon, "Do you find time to pray?
You look so bedraggled, you need to gain weight . . .
But forgive me, Sue Ellen, the hour has grown late.
It's time for five chimes, and I must go to prayer,"
Said Hermione White, as she rose through the air.

It seemed an ascension to Sue Ellen Swallow.
As the great abbey bells rang out clear and true
And upward still upward Hermione flew.
She cooed, "Oh, Great White One, I'm glad I'm like you.
I thank you each day I don't live in a wallow,
With ten shrieking tots like Sue Ellen Swallow.
Her nest is so wooden-frame-church-house and shabby,"
Sang the pompous white pigeon of Whittington Abbey.

Soon the swallow returned to the
Church by the Thames
And flew up under the eaves to her brood.
"Momma, we're hungry," they all chirped at once.
"It's the season of fireflies, please feed us soon.
We've not had a bite since well before noon."

Sue Ellen snared fireflies over the Thames.
She thought of the White One and tried to sing hymns.
But when she opened her beak up to sing,
The fireflies escaped on bright flaming wings.

Sue Ellen quit singing and all through the night
She soared and snared thousands of fireflies in flight.
'Til her nestlings were filled with warm inner light
And started to shine through the deep London night,
Making the city a marvelous sight!
And even Hermione left her high tower
And went to Sue Ellen's that bright midnight hour.

And when she arrived, the White One was there,
And he boomed out, "Hermione, marvel and stare,
And never forget what you see here tonight.
Here, my poor pigeon, is written in light
That swallows in wallows may worship and pray
By caring and loving and serving each day."

Sue Ellen just snuggled down in the nest,
Convinced that the world was her own.
And for the very first time in her gray and black life,
She didn't mind not being white.
For London had learned from one swallow's love
A marvelous lesson of light.

# SLEEVES

Adam and Eve
Didn't have any sleeves
So they found some leaves
And got dressed.
We look like a tree
Said Adam in glee
And we won't have to be
Cleaned or pressed.

## TWEETY-PIE

Sing a song of sixpence
A pocket full of rye,
Four and twenty blackbirds
Baked in a pie.
When the pie was open
The birds began to chirp,
The king looked at his tweety-pie
And said, "I'll skip dessert."

## FRIENDS CAN BE DIFFERENT

They met where they always did
Near the back stairs,
Which were thirty feet up from the
Alley and right.
It was risky to meet in the middle
Of day,
So they had agreed to meet
Only at night.

"Are you there?" Regan called. "Over here,"
Melvin said.
"By the house where the grass was not
Mowed – near the drain!"
So they talked as they always did,
Nearly an hour,
And quietly spoke of life's grief,
Joy and pain.

Each found that the other was one who could share;
Each knew that the other would listen and care.
"Old chum," Regan said, "I don't care what they say,
Life can be big! Friendship can grow in the
Weeds by the house.
It's right to be friends." Regan wistfully said,
Remembering all he had
Shared with the mouse.

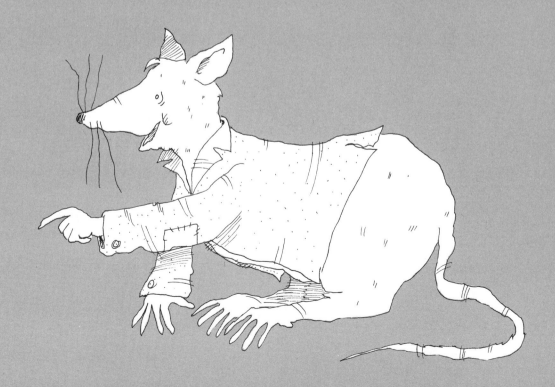

The mouse shook his head,
"Our friendship must end.
There's far too much talk.
The mice that I know
Have firmly closed minds.
We must find our friends among our own kind."

"You are my kind, Melvin. I'm bigger, that's all.
Does it matter so much who's big or who's small?"

"It's not just our size . . . I was high born,
In a fine chest of drawers
And you 'neath the curbing on Hanover Street.
My parents were elegant pantry mice too
And yours rummaged sewers for something to eat."

"When I was a mousling, my mom said to me,
'Melvin, life can be tough:
You will find it a grind
So live tough and think tough and
Stick with your kind.' "
"Must our friendship be over?" The rat
turned away.
"Do you really think, Melvin,
We should end it this way?
Please let's
Meet here at night,
In the weeds by
The house,
To prove
That a rat can be friends
With a mouse."

The fur on his nose was glistening with tears
As Regan walked heavily, feeling his years.

"I'll miss you, old chum, and our long quiet talks,"
He thought as he felt the soft falling of rain;
At the Third Street grating he entered the drain.

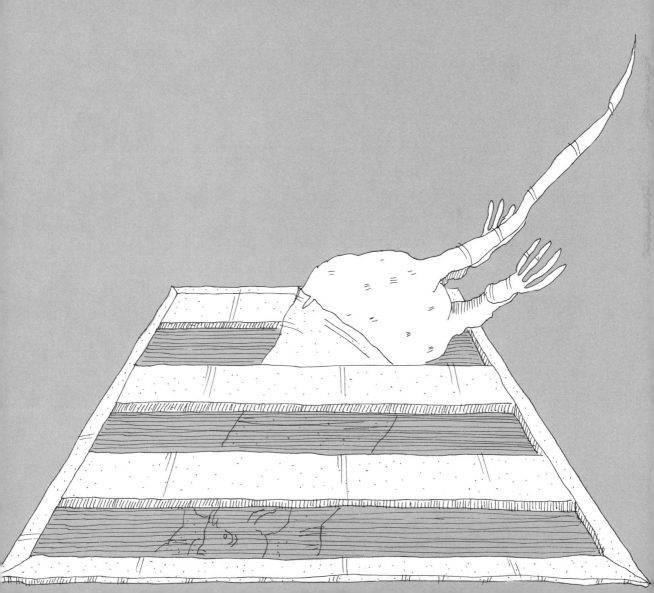

He sloshed along homeward, terribly blue.
At the manhole cover at Fourth Avenue,
He paused in hurt and quiet defeat.
A car roared over the rain-soaked concrete.
He then heard the splashing of four little feet.

"Regan, it's me!" said a voice. "I've been blind.
Friends are forever! I've made up my mind.
We're going to be friends . . . we're two of a kind."

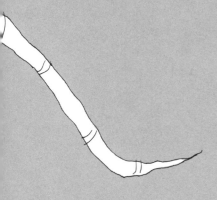

## EATING WITH YOUR EYES OPEN

If a cannibal asks you to dinner don't groan
Just find out if he ends his dinners alone.
Be sure, above all (if dinner's at five),
He has it *all* cooked before you arrive.
Cannibals do have quite excellent taste,
But keep on your side of the table, alert
If your host licks his lips and stares past dessert.
Cannibals are big eaters and terribly strong.
And believe me, their friends never last very long.

# INDEX